CW00554864

Hear The Whispers, Live Your Dream

Hear The Whispers, Live Your Dream

A Fanfare
of Inspiration

Conceived and written by
Andreas Moritz

Ener-chi Wellness Press

Copyright © 2009 by Andreas Moritz, All rights reserved. No part of this publication may be reproduced, stored in a retrieval system, or transmitted in any form or by any means, electronic, mechanical, photocopying, recording or otherwise, without the prior written permission of the copyright owner.

ISBN-13: 978-09821801-5-0

Published by Ener-Chi Wellness Press —
Ener-Chi.com, USA
Printed by Lightning Source Inc, USA

Cover Design and Artwork by Andreas Moritz
The picture on the cover is part of *Ener-Chi Art* (see http://.ener-chi.com), designed to increase Chi flow in all organs and systems of the body. This particular picture is designed to enhance general health of mind, body and spirit.

The message by Solomon at the end of the book was specifically channeled for the readers of this book through Lily, one of the world's most gifted inter-dimensional communicators. For more information about Lily and her services, please visit http://acrossdimensions.com.

Open up your heart
like a flower in the sun

↓

Ask a question
in your mind

↓

Open this book to any page
and receive your answer with

gratitude

Contents

Part One

Body
Awareness
Affirmations

Life has taught me that being overly
health conscious stems from the
belief in disease.
The belief in disease further
prevents me from being well and
whole.
By allowing myself to be who I am
and forsaking all ideas of who I
should be, restores me to my center.
I realize that I can only heal or be
whole again when I am in my center.

Healing is effortless. I cannot force
the body to heal.
The power of healing can only act
when I move out of its way.
Healing is allowing.
Sickness is resisting.

When I become ill, I don't panic but
know something beneficial is
happening to me.
I recognize the illness is not
accidental but occurs to help me
come face to face with issues I am not
aware of, or not in harmony with.
To heal, I open my heart to these
unresolved issues by breathing them
into me with gratitude.

Instead of asking what harm the disease causes me, I ask how it serves me to have this disease?
Feeling ill, I do not see myself as being weak. Instead I see the strength and courage
in it—to allow such a limiting condition to come into my life so that I can learn from it and grow even stronger because of it.
Foremost of all, I don't see myself as being a victim.

I give my body the loving attention it
deserves and cannot be without.
With vibrant health and joyful
sensations, my body responds to all
my needs and wants.
A temple of God, my body is my
playfield of all possibilities.

I treat my body like I would treat my lover or best friend.
I give it the very best of everything: fresh and wholesome food; a soothing, clean environment; comfortable clothing; uplifting sounds and colors; and, foremost of all, loving gratitude for all it is doing for me.

My body serves as a clean, well-circulated and oxygen-rich home for the trillions of cells that depend on me for their life.
How I breathe, sleep, eat, think and act determines how my body is able to perform.

Harmful microorganisms cannot survive in my body, and disease is naturally absent.
Bacteria and viruses become my enemies only if I fear, resist or fight them.
'Love thy enemies' or 'resist nothing' is my preferred approach to healing an illness, shall the need arise.
I now realize that what I resist persists.

My body is cleansing itself of toxins and congestion, and I fully support that effort.
I nourish my body through foods, thoughts and feelings that are of the highest vibration.
Each cell of my body is bathed in the joy of being loved and, therefore, is able to serve its unique purpose.

As I am aligning my purpose and existence with the Earth's purpose and existence, I will begin to enjoy perfect, unending health and youthfulness, in body, mind and spirit.

My genetic material is of a crystalline substance that has the power to transmute anything my body does not need or want.
The crystalline substance of my own subtle bodies made of light can permeate the molecular structure of any base particles and reassemble them into crystalline purity.

When my body sustains a wound, the
electrical current between the site of
the injury and the surrounding tissue
remains high, so my body can quickly
and thoroughly
heal itself.

I trust that my body always knows what to do at any given moment. As long as I don't succumb to fear and doubt, it will continue to serve me on my spiritual journey of awakening. All I am asked to do is maintain body awareness. I set aside enough time to give my body the loving time and attention it requires to guide me and safely lead me through the jungle of life.

My genes are an intrinsic part of my existence, and they have no separate agenda. They merely act as blueprints to reproduce the beautiful cells of my body. By virtue of being conscious, I am the one who creates the blueprints anew each day.
I know that what I do, eat, drink, feel and think determines how well my genes are able to control and maintain my physical existence.

Words and the way we say them are powerful healing tools. I use the Primordial Sounds hidden in the words of the spoken language to restore and sustain the original genetic blueprint and functions of my tissues, organs and systems.
These sounds derive their healing power from the force of love and compassion I direct to all of creation, including myself.

The vital energy contained in the food I eat is essential for my wellbeing. I seek to eat only foods that are fresh and full of vitality. Moreover, I seek to breathe fresh air filled with vital energy. I surround myself with clean air so that I may remain connected with the natural world and never feel separate from it.

I have learned that a disease cannot be its own cause and, therefore, cannot be cured by merely removing its symptoms.
By treating the symptoms of an illness, its causes remain or become more severe. This may lead to increasingly persistent symptoms in the future.
I see illness to be a healing mechanism of the body, which deserves my complete support.

The most effective way of dealing with disease is to remove any energy-depleting factors that may impede the body's ever-present effort to return to its natural state of balance or equilibrium.

Overeating, poor nutrition, lack of sleep, not drinking enough fresh water, use of pharmaceutical drugs and stimulants, not expressing emotions, etc., deplete the body's energy reserves and render it susceptible to disease-causing reasons.

By cleansing my body from accumulated waste material and toxins, and by establishing a healthy diet and lifestyle, I create the preconditions for the body to heal itself, effortlessly and without much discomfort.

Not a single idea, thought or desire, positive or negative, can run through my mind without also generating a corresponding powerful biochemical reaction in every cell of my body. My body acts like a recording device that records everything I see, hear, touch, smell and taste.   And it plays back these recordings in due time so that I may learn and grow from all my creations.

Part Two

Perception &
Choice
Affirmations

I place a value on everything in my life,
regardless whether events are
positive or negative.
This way, my life is full excitement
and abundance; everything becomes
valuable and nothing is left useless.

To achieve perfection in life, I do not need to do anything but accept what is.

Trying to accomplish what 'should be' is mere denial of my current reality. By propelling myself into a fictitious future, I only separate myself from the present, which prevents me from fulfilling my desires.

By accepting whatever happens to me, I am actively involved in the outcome of my thoughts and feelings.

I realize that I am everything that I
seek and perceive—no less, no more.
The way I perceive things is up to me,
and not to the things I perceive.
Since perception shapes reality,
I choose to embrace all of life,
regardless how it presents itself
to me.

The solution to my problems is not outside me; I am that solution. If I perceive a situation to be a problem instead of a gift or blessing, I do not need to solve the problem, but adjust my perception of it.

Perception is one of the most powerful forces in my life. It shapes my personal reality. Since I can choose to see things the way I want to, I can also create my reality in any way I want to.

There is no power that controls my life other than the way I perceive myself and the world. Everything depends on it.

I do not use hope as a way of life, for this would imply that I am in denial of what is and wish for something else to be in its place.

My acceptance of whatever occurs at each moment, is the only objective and realistic way of life.

By leaving out the judgment of what it *should* be, I am in the truth of the matter. I AM.

I am also centered in my power. This is the basis of meaningful and buoyant creativity.

It is becoming increasingly obvious to me that when I accept each moment as it is, without blaming or criticizing myself or others, and without hope that it may change, then the floodgates of love, life and abundance will open fully to me. And I will understand each moment's uniqueness and perfection, and be grateful for it.

Whenever appropriate, I give myself permission to let things go and leave things be the way they are, especially if they appear to be confused, out of control and in disarray.
I give up the need to fix everything that I think needs fixing.

Worries are unnecessary. They reflect the perception that something bad is happening, whereas bad things show that something good is happening: old things are clearing and new things are emerging.
Worries attach us to old things and keep them in place, which merely gives rise to more worries.
Obstacles in life are merely blessings that offer us a way out of undesirable situations.

I also allow myself to do things that do not have a purpose, simply because I feel like it.
Likewise, I let other people do what they like, even if I believe they are mistaken or wasting their time.
I realize that while trying new things I will inevitably make mistakes, which forms an important part of the process of learning. There really are no mistakes.

I have consciously forsaken to be on a program of self-improvement, for this would imply I do not accept who I am. Not accepting who I am forms the basis of being self-critical and judgmental, and, in turn, creates inner turmoil and unhappiness.
Instead, I now make being love, peace and happiness the main reason behind all my activities. If love, peace and happiness remain elusive in my life, I recognize that my focus has been on making these my goal rather than being them.

It is becoming increasingly clear to me
that my true Self has no limitations; it
has no permanent identity that moves
in linear sequence from birth to
death.
Time for me is eternity.
I am like the clear sky through which
blow all the winds of creation. Even
when the winds stop blowing, I will still
be there.

I know that enlightenment, or ascension to an exalted form of existence, is but the simple acceptance of each moment as being perfect, especially when it brings things into my life that are anything but perfect.

It is my expectancy that makes things appear to be good and bad, right and wrong, pleasing or distressing.

My perception of perfection makes it real.

My intent makes me get up in the
morning, wash my body, exercise and
eat a nourishing meal.
I use the same power of intention to
fulfill all my other desires.
I recognize that those desires that
remain unfulfilled do not need to
come to fruition for a good reason.

I have always had the dream to change the world. I now know I cannot change it unless I see myself through the eyes of love and acceptance. I have learned that I need not become a different person to help this world. I am here to love myself for who I am, regardless of my flaws and weaknesses. By doing so, the world has already become a better place.

It is not my job to make the world to be just as I want it. Rather, I allow the world as others choose to see it, to exist as well.

However, I make it my business to love the world I create around me. How much I love myself determines how deeply I will able to love others, the world around me, the creatures of nature, even my chosen God.

I see the world as an exciting,
challenging place that has the
enormous potential of becoming a
paradise in my lifetime.
With the number of problems
increasing, we are also given an equal
number of solutions.
With each problem solved, we
experience a rise in frequency that
brings us a step closer to manifesting
a loving planetary home
that we all deserve.

While others see doom and gloom in
the world's affairs, I see its potential
and the loss of only what is
no longer needed.
I see that death gives rise to birth.
For the whole world to become a
paradise, the balance must be tipped,
the climates change, the elements be
purified. For the new world to
emerge, the old one must die. Giving
birth may be a painful experience, but
it also a celebration of new life.

When I think of death, I am
immediately reminded of Rumi's
precious words:
"On the day I die, when I'm being
carried toward the grave, don't weep.
Don't say, She's gone! She's gone.
Death has nothing to do with going
away. The sun sets and the moon
sets, but they're not gone. Death is a
coming together. The tomb looks like
a prison, but it's really release into
union. The human seed goes down in
the ground like a bucket into the well
where Joseph is. It grows and comes
up full of some unimagined beauty.
Your mouth closes here
and immediately opens
with a shout of joy there."

Perception shapes reality.
The network of nerves in my brain stem—my traffic control center—only permits life-enhancing messages to enter my conscious mind because I decide so.
This allows me to comprehend what the real world looks like, sounds like and feels like.

If I so will, I can use 100% of my heart and brain capacity at all times. Seeing myself as weak, unworthy, poor, ill, victimized, mistreated or otherwise not in control, merely shuts down my heart, greatly limits my brain capacity and materializes my fears. The secret key to living my full potential and fulfilling all my dreams is to fully accept myself the way I am. I am in divine perfection.

I have made oneness the priority in my life. I see it in every stone, the dirt, the insects, the clouds, the rain, the sun, in others and myself.
This fills me up with love and compassion for all that is, regardless of who or what it is.

I have a spiritual purpose in my life.
Naturally, everything I do is a means
to enhance the variations of bliss in
my life and in the world.

In the years ahead, many on this
Earth will come to the realization that
no life form needs to earn
the right to live.
The fact of its existence is enough
proof that it has the right to exist and
be treated with love,
compassion and respect.

I know that abundance cannot be
measured by how many possessions I
have accumulated, or how much
power and wealth I have in my name.
My wealth is measured by
how good I feel about myself,
others and the world.

It is quite unimportant what others think of me, but it is important what I think of them.

If I yearn for another's recognition, I will depend on them for my sense of worthiness.

If I give recognition to another, my heart will expand and be filled with joy.

I open the floodgate of abundance
by being a channel for the abundance
in the universe.
I recognize that poverty is only my
resistance to accept abundance into
my life or to feel deserving of it. The
streams of abundance are always
present and will never dry out,
regardless of whether I resist or
accept them.
The universe assumes that whatever
I put my attention on is what I want;
so it graciously provides me with more
of the same.

The gratitude I feel for all the things that I have in my life begets more of the same. Thus, the stream of limitless abundance is impossible to stop, as long as I remain grateful for what I have.

As my trust in the laws of give and take increases, I see that the more I give from my heart, the more I receive an abundance of love, joy, appreciation, opportunities and material wealth.
I further realize that money and possessions are not the cause but the effect of abundance in my life.

My ability to let go of my attachment to anything I own bestows freedom on me—the freedom to give and receive whatever I need to achieve a higher purpose in life.

True abundance is the complete trust that I am at the right place at the right time. I know that I am and always will be connected to the river of life, which knows all my needs and desires wherever I am and whatever I do.

This is my wellspring of abundance.

I know that there is nothing in this
universe that is useless or void of
specific meaning or purpose.
I also know that nothing can ever
happen to me that is not in my best
interest, even if it leaves me confused
or in pain.

There are no negative versus
positive events, people or situations
in my life.
My perception of whatever comes
into my life is shaped by the
expectancy that it must be a gift; and
so it is.

When things seem difficult, I remind myself of what Sir Winston Churchill once said:
"A pessimist sees the difficulty in every opportunity; and the optimist sees the opportunity in every difficulty."

I know that everyone, no matter what
the circumstances or appearance may
be, is a God in embryo ready to be
born.
I recognize that people are not the
masks they wear or the roles they
play without knowing what they do.
When I pass judgment on them I only
pass judgment on myself.

I know that any difficulties I face in my life conceal a deeper purpose that is there to help me grow stronger and wiser than I am. It is up to me to decipher and use them for the enhancement of my personal growth. Removing the rocks along my path only makes my muscles stronger and helps me build my life in a more fulfilling way than I can imagine.

I am learning to not define my life by what happens around me.
If the world is tumultuous, I can be still. I can be well. If life is bumpy, I can be steadfast. If disaster strikes, I can be well.
My wellbeing does not depend on how the world is treating me, but on how I treat the world.
For as long as I give love, no harm can truly reach me.

I let life reflect me so I can see my inner light reflected by everything and everyone I see.

If someone is unkind to me, I see this to be an opportunity to retaliate with extra kindness. I do not let others' rudeness enter my heart, but instead open my heart to them to see their pain, fear and sadness.

The compassion that fills my heart changes their attitude toward me and helps them feel better about themselves.

There is a larger picture at work in my life. In this larger picture, I am always protected and never alone. If nobody cares about me, I can still care about myself. If nobody respects me, I can still respect myself. If nobody loves me, I can still love myself.

Without caring about, respecting and loving myself, I would be truly insecure and lonely, even if the whole world were there to care about, respect and love me.

I welcome, accept, celebrate and express gratitude for everything that is and the way it is.
I choose joy in everything I do, for joy is my anchor to the one and only source of life.
If I find myself doing something out of fear, I wait until joy becomes the motivation for my actions once again.

I now know that any obstacles or negative situations in my life are, in fact, blessings in disguise that serve as unique opportunities for me to become more complete and whole inside, and to move forward in life. Seeing them for what they truly are opens the door to the abundance of love, freedom, health, joy, wealth and unlimited possibilities.

Whatever I resist persists.
When something does not seem to please me, I notice my resistance that keeps it that way. The more resistance I put up to things or people in my life, the stronger the reasons for my resistance become. I am stuck with whatever I despise until I become thankful for what has come my way. As I replace my resistance with acceptance of what is, I can transform what I do not like into something that I do like.

I recognize that my problems and inadequacies are also my best guides and teachers.
I am always safe because, like everything in this universe, I am God also.
I am one with everything, so there is nothing I need to be afraid of and nothing that can really harm me.

I have agreed to everything that happens to me, for my own good. And so I look at setbacks as wake-up calls, as timely opportunities for positive change and growth.

I am not trapped by the illusion that
something starts at one particular
time and ends some time later.
I realize that time has no beginning
and no end. It simply is eternal. All
events are seamlessly interwoven. At
any moment, while in the present, I
can be in any time in the future or any
time in the past, depending on what I
choose to see or be.
I accept each new moment to be the
most perfect moment it can be.

There is no gap between past and present, or present and the future, except in my mind. The events of a past or future life are happening right now in a parallel form of reality. Nothing in life can come to an end or be lost. Therefore, the wise ones who live throughout all time do not mourn over what has come to pass, or fear what is yet to come.

I keep my attention on every new moment as it slips into the presence of my experience.
In so doing, I become the master of time, and am able to live my life to the fullest, without fear of future or past events.

I know that I am truly one with the
spirit, essence or source of
everything that exists.
I can instantly create anything I wish
for in my mind. As the illusion of my
separateness from the natural world
and from time dissipates, my mental
creations become physical reality.

I value and respect myself and all life around me. Therefore, I receive the spontaneous support of all the laws of nature.
All my needs are taken care of automatically, before I can wish for them.

Those persons with whom I have the greatest difficulties are the ones who give me the best opportunity to undo the hard knots of my karma.
Karma is not a form of punishment or sin, but rather gift packets we have given to ourselves to help remove the armor of false protection from our hearts.

I know that I am, and always will be,
connected to the river of life. It knows
all my needs and desires, wherever I
shall be and whatever I will do.
I profoundly trust that the river of life
will always flow in the right direction,
even when it moves in a winding
course. Its many twists and turns
makes my life exciting and worth
living.

I realize that I have created a unique way of living in order to learn the virtues of unconditional love, patience, forgiveness, compassion, service and acceptance. Accordingly, I am being presented with all kinds of 'adverse' situations until I have fully and comfortably mastered these precious virtues.

I know that silence is the dynamic
power that propels all activity. It
keeps my body sound and healthy,
and my mind clear and alert.
I therefore choose to consciously
experience the periods of silence
between the periods of activity,
whenever the opportunity arises.

I place attention on the underlying oneness that connects me to all people, all objects and all of nature. I recognize that there is a greater purpose in all that happens to me and that the river of life flows through me and all of creation. This deep connection makes all forms of life equally important, useful and valuable.

We literally imprint our feelings, and emotions on objects such as chairs, cars and houses. I may walk into the house of a complete stranger, and yet it may feel like home. It feels like home because the people living in it radiate peacefulness and happiness into every nook and cranny of their home.

I treat every object I touch or come into contact with as kindly and respectfully as I can. Thus, in my own little ways, I am able to spread some more kindness in this world.

I realize that the power that runs my life and the power that run the universe are the same. When I desire things that are in harmony and in synch with the world, there can be no power to prevent the fulfillment of my dreams.

I do not base my existence on the illusion of losses and gains, for in truth, nothing can be lost, and nothing can be gained. I only lose what is no longer of use to me, and what I gain does not add more value to who I already am. I remain who I am regardless what I lose or gain in life.

When I enter into this world, I arrive
with nothing except myself, and when
I depart from it, I leave with nothing
but myself. I existed before I was
born, and I continue to exist after I
leave my physical body behind. Life
neither begins with birth, nor does it
end with death. The world may come,
and the world may go, but I will go on
forever.

When nothing can be gained and nothing can be lost, why fuss over either gain or loss? As always, when one door closes, another one opens. This is the cycle of eternal life.

I do not require manmade rules, regulations or belief systems to know what is right for me. I am no longer bound by beliefs that are based on fear and other negative expectations. I only allow into my life what excites me and brings me joy; and I let go of what doesn't.

I know that fearful thoughts can lead
to an avalanche of fear, and cause
chaos and confusion all around me.
Instead of letting fear be my guide, I
guide myself *through* the fear and
facing and transcending it with love,
trust and courage.

I know that Mother Earth is a
conscious being and is evolving just
as we are. By entering the
frequencies of higher dimensions, she
is rising above the thought forms of
right and wrong, victim and victimizer,
abused and abuser. Our planet is
letting go of duality consciousness.
I am also evolving to embrace my own
higher dimensions of consciousness.
This is a natural cosmic event and is
in the best interests of Mother
Earth and all beings.

There can be great purpose in our "mistakes" if we understand their meaning. The problems they create persist until we find the meaning or true purpose that is hidden within them.

I make it a point to bless whatever happens to me and consciously attach meaning to it. That meaning becomes the reality I accept and remember.

My attitude toward problems is a friendly one because they could turn out to be the best teachers I have ever had.

I am willing to acknowledge and understand the reasons behind all my resistance to people, problems and situations. I know that they are only exist to teach me the lesson of love and raise my consciousness to a level where spiritual wisdom will become my daily experience and heartfelt reality.

I forsake the need for positive
thinking to quell negative thoughts.
Ignored or suppressed negative
thoughts and feelings turn into
poisons that then require serious
purging from the body and mind.
Instead, I ignore or repress nothing at
all, but embrace and touch everything
I resist with the flames of my love.
I honor, welcome and accept all my
thoughts, feelings, emotions and
actions, no matter how unpleasant or
painful they may appear to be.

I pass along loving thoughts, friendly gestures and encouraging words to everyone I meet. I do this for the joy of doing it and expect nothing in return.
Whatever I might receive in return would never be more fulfilling than the joy I've already found.

I realize there cannot be lasting
happiness for anyone in our world
unless poverty, starvation, conflict,
war, illness, and destruction of the
environment are completely rooted
out everywhere.
To whatever extent I am able to, and
through my own small sphere of
expertise and influence, I strive to
help others find their path, passion,
and fulfillment just as I am seeking
my own.

Like my body, our planet, Mother Earth (Gaia), was designed to go through times of upheaval and healing crises. These help correct the imbalances superimposed on her by the human race. The crises trigger powerful responses by her immune system.

Instead of burdening Gaia with more fear and worry, I infuse her with my love and admiration for all the amazing things she still does for all of us.

The ever-increasing and unpredictable fluctuations of temperature and climate are merely cleansing procedures, initiated by Gaia in coordination with Sun activities. Mother Earth is acting to rid herself off all the stress, tension and pollution caused by human beings over a long period of time. In whatever way I can, I am committed to treat Gaia as I would treat my mother.

I know that every so often the best
things in life come disguised as
misfortunes. These misfortunes
merely represent tests of whether I
am ready and welcoming enough to
receive the blessings they
bring along.

Everything that I do to assist my body and increase its purity is a love gift to the universe, my Higher Self. I cleanse my organs of impurities, feed my body well with natural foods and give it sufficient rest. I treat every part of my body with utmost respect and it rewards me with joy, happiness and radiant vitality.
And if I neglect or fail to do so today, I will love myself a little more tomorrow.

I know that there is no motivation on behalf of the spiritual universe to support desires that do not serve the whole.
I also realize that material wealth is highly volatile. Spiritual wealth, however, is stable, boundless and inexhaustible and takes care of my material needs, no matter how adverse the circumstances.

Many human beings are in the
process of awakening to the
realization that we actually deserve
the very best of everything because
we are one with everything.
This means that whatever belongs to
others also belongs to me; and
whatever is mine, is theirs, too.
If I steal from others I actually steal
from myself. If I give to others, I also
gift myself.

My consciousness or spirit is the
only true source of the energy and
information that runs my body.
I am fully aware that I am a spiritual
being that lives in and expresses itself
through a physical body. Hence, my
primary needs are of a spiritual
nature, and not a physical one.
I don't look for physical pleasure or
gratification unless it also enriches
my spiritual essence.

I know that all of life's problems exist
only to teach me the lesson of love
and raise my consciousness to a level
where spiritual wisdom can become
my daily experience and reality.
The seeds of love have begun to
sprout and raise the vibrations of my
body, mind and spirit.

My Higher Self knows exactly what
learning opportunities I need, so that
I can evolve toward greater wisdom,
love and empowerment, however hard
and painful the learning process may
appear to be.

My Higher Self sometimes puts
obstacles in my way so that I may
develop the qualities of courage,
strength, love, confidence and
wisdom to the fullest extent possible.

This also means that nothing can
ever be wrong with me.

Part Three

Manifestation
Affirmations

If I get upset about something that happens to me, I am aware that it is not the actual event or striation that disturbs me, but the thoughts and reactions I have about it.
I therefore chose not to change the situation itself but rather my perception of it. This way, I don't need to fear or fight it, and be at peace.

My human DNA has upgraded
itself to twelve or more strands.
Many brain cells that had been lying
dormant are now completely awake.
I am now using the full potential of my
physical body and brain, which
enables me to live in a higher
dimension of reality.

I realize the power of creation vested in me. Whenever I think of or imagine something, I create a new reality which cannot be undone. How I respond to my creation determines how it will affect my life.
I am profoundly inspired by the following words of wisdom:

—

"Imagination is everything. It is the preview of life's coming attractions."
~Albert Einstein

—

"Whatever the mind of man can conceive, it can achieve."
~W. Clement Stone

It is the infinite wisdom of my Higher Self—intrinsically one with the infinite wisdom that runs the universe—that generates inner guidance.

My Higher Self always knows what is good for me at every moment, and this includes making what appear to be mistakes or facing an impediment.

My happiness has begun to grow rapidly, since I foster those desires that help and support my extended self—the human race, the animals and nature, the Earth, the Sun and the universe.

I am the only one that creates
my reality.
I am the master of my destiny, and I
decree that every moment in my life is
a divine moment, blessed with
momentous opportunities for growth,
learning and new possibilities.

I recognize that love, honesty and trust are the only necessary and effective means of success in life, including the creation of perfect health, abundance and spiritual wisdom.

But I also know that experiencing fear, dishonesty and lack of confidence in myself can serve as stepping stones toward manifesting their opposite qualities. Therefore, I see them as blessings to achieve even greater gifts.

Luck comes to me automatically
because I have no doubt about my
own power to achieve what I want and
what I need.
I have no doubt that whatever
happens to me is in my best interest.
This is what I call luck.

I know that seeing something as negative is caused by not perceiving its opposite positive counterpart. Therefore, there is not a single space left in my mind to entertain purely negative thoughts. Accordingly, I receive many more opportunities for growth, success and happiness than I have ever had before.

I freely give something to someone each day. I do not expect anything in return, not even a well wishing thought or gesture. This helps me get in touch with the deepest aspects of myself, which are all based on oneness. I know that everything I do for others, I am actually doing for myself.

My power is infinite because I am one
with everything.
I no longer allow my power to be
dispersed by permitting other
people's beliefs and opinions to rule
my life. I rely on my own knowledge
and understanding, but I am open to
learning from everyone I meet and
every situation that presents itself
to me.

Even though the Earth is huge, it revolves around the Sun in perfect silence. Likewise, flowers and trees make no sound when they grow. All activities accompanied by silence are perfect. By making this principle my own, I have witnessed my own personal world being transformed into a state of permanent grace.

I give my loving attention to nature and receive her love back a million-fold. Mother Earth is eager to give untold abundance to those who love and respect her.

Whenever I gently touch a flower or tree, or when I whisper sweet nothings to an insect landing on my hand, or when I see the enormous contribution a simple microbe makes to all life, the entire world is being informed I am a friend of the Earth.

I am an unbounded field of creative
power that is ready to be used for
the purpose of creating and enjoying
Heaven on Earth.
The tools of this creative power are
my thoughts and feelings. Since no
one else can think or feel for me, I am
the only creator of my reality.

I prefer to learn things in a spontaneous, effortless way, just as I did when I was a young child. Increasingly, I perceive the world in its higher dimensional reality, where thoughts become instantly fulfilled.

The now greatly intensified energies
of the sun are raising planetary
vibrations to such high levels that
almost everyone on the planet will be
motivated only by love.
This process becomes accelerated
when we no longer fear the sun, but
let it shine on our skin and heal our
body, mind and heart.

I focus on perfect health, abundant
energy, renewed creativity and
spiritual ripening so I spontaneously
manifest these qualities in my life.
There are no other influences on my
body or mind, other than those that I
allow and create through my own
awareness.
Whatever occurs in my mind is bound
to manifest somewhere and sometime
in my life.

Each of my thoughts—positive and
negative—creates a life on its own.
This makes me a master of my
destiny, one way or the other.
By becoming still, I naturally take my
attention away from what I don't
want, and place it on what I wish to
know and become.
Being anchored in the stillness of my
being, I am able to create whatever
my heart desires.

According to the law 'like attracts like,' the thoughts I think today beget similar thoughts tomorrow.
I no longer choose to think of the glass being half empty, but now choose to see it half full. While I may not be able to change a situation right now, by seeing it from this new abundant perspective, it will surely be different.

I know that true prayer is the
expressing of gratitude for what has
already occurred. Gratitude is
positive energy that attracts and
increases more of
what I am grateful for.

Problems abound when there is fear.
Problems are absent when there is
love.
I vibrate at a high frequency of love,
not fear, and so I create solutions to
problems with lightning speed.

I trust that whatever I can imagine is also real. It must be real because I created it. Thoughts are the driving force behind every human achievement.

I prefer to focus my thoughts and feelings on what works well in my life than on what does not work. This keeps me receptive to and deserving of new opportunities, joy and abundance.

Instead of observing or pointing out what I dislike in others, I rather dwell on what I like about myself. This enables me to perceive the same beautiful qualities in others as well, even if it's just in potential form.

The thoughts I think create my personal reality. They reflect how I feel about myself. How I feel about myself is a choice I need to make at every moment. This is not as difficult as it sounds since there is nobody else responsible for how I treat myself, regardless of how I was treated in the past.

As my self worthiness and self-appreciation increases, the wealth and abundance present in every nook and cranny of the universe is being directed towards me.
What others think of me is none of my business. I realize that it benefits nobody if I make it my business.

I talk to and treat the cells of my
body as if they were my best friends.
Since I am in perfect touch with all
the cells in my body, I receive from
them waves of blissful well- being
that makes me feel loved,
whole and healthy.

I always expect the best things to happen in my life and, therefore, I am certain they will manifest in one form or another.
And since I believe everything I experience to be a blessing,, even if it doesn't seem that way, my life is and remains perfect for the rest of my time.

If I think thoughts of illness and lack, I manifest disease and poverty. If think thoughts of health and prosperity, I will be healthy and prosperous.
I do not try to think positive thoughts, for they merely mask the negative ones. Instead, I choose to think what I love to be or have in my life, while being mindless to what I do not have.

I know that when I give something to
someone with all my heart, without
conditions or expectations, I also
draw abundance to myself
in many forms.
By genuinely wishing others to have
an abundance of love, health and joy,
I automatically grow more abundant
with those same gifts.

When one of my desires does not become fulfilled, I know that one of two things has occurred:
(1) I internalized a doubt, which had a sabotaging effect on fulfilling the desire; or,
(2) my desire was not in harmony with the greater purpose of my life or my surroundings.
In any case, I do not feel disappointed because all is well the way it is right at this moment.

Each moment, I strive to serve my heart, my body, my fellow humans, the animals, the plants, all life forms and the planet as a whole, in the best ways I can. By doing so, I intensify the power of love in and around me. This is the most important work that I can do in my life. It is the primary purpose of my presence here on Earth. Whatever else I do is relatively insignificant.

I know I do not become strong by
seeking those situations that make
me feel secure and protected.
I become strong by navigating
through all kinds of storms, and
finding my direction and purpose
from within.

There are no other influences on my body, other than the ones I create or allow through my own awareness.
I create what I fear, but I also create what I love. I prefer to create through love than through fear.

I know that whatever I need to live comfortably and joyfully, will land at my doorstep, somehow, someway, someday.
But I also know I need to be vigilant, and open the door when I hear it knock. Many waste their life by waiting for the big day that everything will change for them, and so nothing ever changes.
I have learned to welcome everything that happens to me. If something seems unpleasant to me, by accepting it anyway, it will reveal to me its pleasant side.

I feel gratitude for the difficult times in my life. They give me the opportunity to grow stronger and wiser.
I have learned valuable lessons from my mistakes.
When I am grateful for my troubles, they inevitably turn into blessings.
Such is the power of manifestation.

I am a member of co-creation, and
everything that happens to me is in
my favor, even if think it is not.
I know that whatever meaning I attach
to an event or situation, ends up as
my truth and reality. Therefore, I
consciously choose to see everything
as a blessing. So be it, and so it is.

I know that every war and conflict the Earth has ever witnessed and still experiences, comes from our resistance to accepting one another the way we are, with all our unique differences, apparent faults and wondrous assets.

Illness is a sign of fragmentation and separation. Health is the manifestation of wholeness or oneness of all the parts. Appreciating the cells of my body for their incessant work and love for me is a powerful secret of healing, because the vibration of 'Thank You' connects what has been separated.

My karma's sole purpose is to restore the "lost" awareness of oneness. This makes karma's role an important one.
Because I am here, I am also important, just as every one else is. I am here to help restore the oneness that seems amiss.

I am perfectly capable of blessing all things with my spiritual essence. It is not my job to fix the problems of the world, but to let my love, compassion and joy shine unto them. Increasing my happiness and letting it radiate is my purpose in life. This is my mission.

<u>Words of Wisdom by Rumi</u>

I swear my dear son
no one in the entire world
is as precious as you are

look at that mirror
take a good look at yourself
who else is there above and beyond
you

now give yourself a kiss
and with sweet whispers
fill your ears to the brim

watch for all that beauty
reflecting from you
and sing a love song to your
existence

you can never overdo
praising your own soul
you can never over-pamper your
heart

you are both
the father and the son
the sugar and the sugar cane

who else but you
please tell me who else
can ever take your place

now give yourself a smile

what is the worth of a diamond
if it doesn't shine

how can I ever put a price
on the diamond that you are
you are the entire treasure of the
house

you and your shadow
are forever present in this world
you're that glorious bird of paradise

Channeled Inspiration
By LilY

Put faith in the knowingness that all is
well and worthy in your life. You are
at one with all the heavens and can
bask in the dance of the ages, for
today and tomorrow meld into the
now of yesterday in the blink
of an eye.
Capture each moment, each blessing
beat of the now, and know you are an
integral part of it. The Allness That
Is is enhanced by your
magnificent presence and glows with
the lamplight of your heart's fire and
desires.
Be not separated from your
thoughts of selfness and oneness for
they are the same. We are all
entwined in the dance of love where
fate holds untold truths for us to
reap and celebrate.

Breathe deeply of the love in the air
that surrounds you and rejoice in the
knowing that you are giving so much
to this planet's beauty and vitality.
So take also – drink deeply and
continuously from the chalice of life
and share your gifts with all those
around you.
Simply by *being* you fulfill your role
and purpose in the truest sense. Do
not doubt your value or your
contributions so long as you come
from a place of heart, for there is no
greater gift or accomplishment than
being in the light of love.

~Solomon *(channeled by Lily ~
5.10.09)*

Also by Andreas Moritz

· · ·

The Amazing Liver and Gallbladder Flush

Timeless Secrets of Health and Rejuvenation

Cancer is Not a Disease – It's a Survival Mechanism

Lifting the Veil of Duality

It's Time to Come Alive

Simple Steps to Total Health

Heart Disease No More!

Diabetes – No More!

Ending the AIDS Myth

Heal Yourself with Sunlight

Sacred Santémony & Ener-Chi Art

All books are available at
www.ener-chi.com, **www.amazon.com**, and
other online or physical bookstores

ABOUT THE AUTHOR

Andreas Moritz is one of the world's leading experts on Integrative Medicine. He is a medical intuitive; a practitioner of Ayurveda, iridology, shiatsu, and vibrational medicine; a writer; and an artist. Born in southwest Germany in 1954, Moritz had to deal with several severe illnesses from an early age, which compelled him to study diet, nutrition, and various methods of natural healing while still a child.

Rather than being satisfied with merely treating the symptoms of illness, Moritz has dedicated his life's work to understanding and treating the root causes of illness. Because of this holistic approach, he has had great success with cases of terminal disease where conventional methods of healing proved futile. His books and other healing modalities made available through this site are designed to help a person address the root causes of ill health and naturally support the body's own healing abilities.

For more information about
Andreas, Moritz, his telephone
consultation service, his other books,
Ener-Chi Art, Sacred Santémony,
Ionized Stones and other products,
please visit:

http://ener-chi.com

Tollfree ordering
(1)866-258-4006 (USA)

Local
(1)709-570-7401 (Canada)

Lightning Source UK Ltd.
Milton Keynes UK

171187UK00001B/32/P